AF580444

ISBN: 978-1-7339066-1-6

Published by HavenLight
380 E. 620 S Ste. B
American Fork, UT 84003
www.HavenLight.com

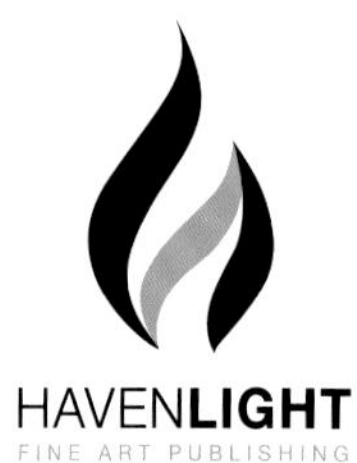

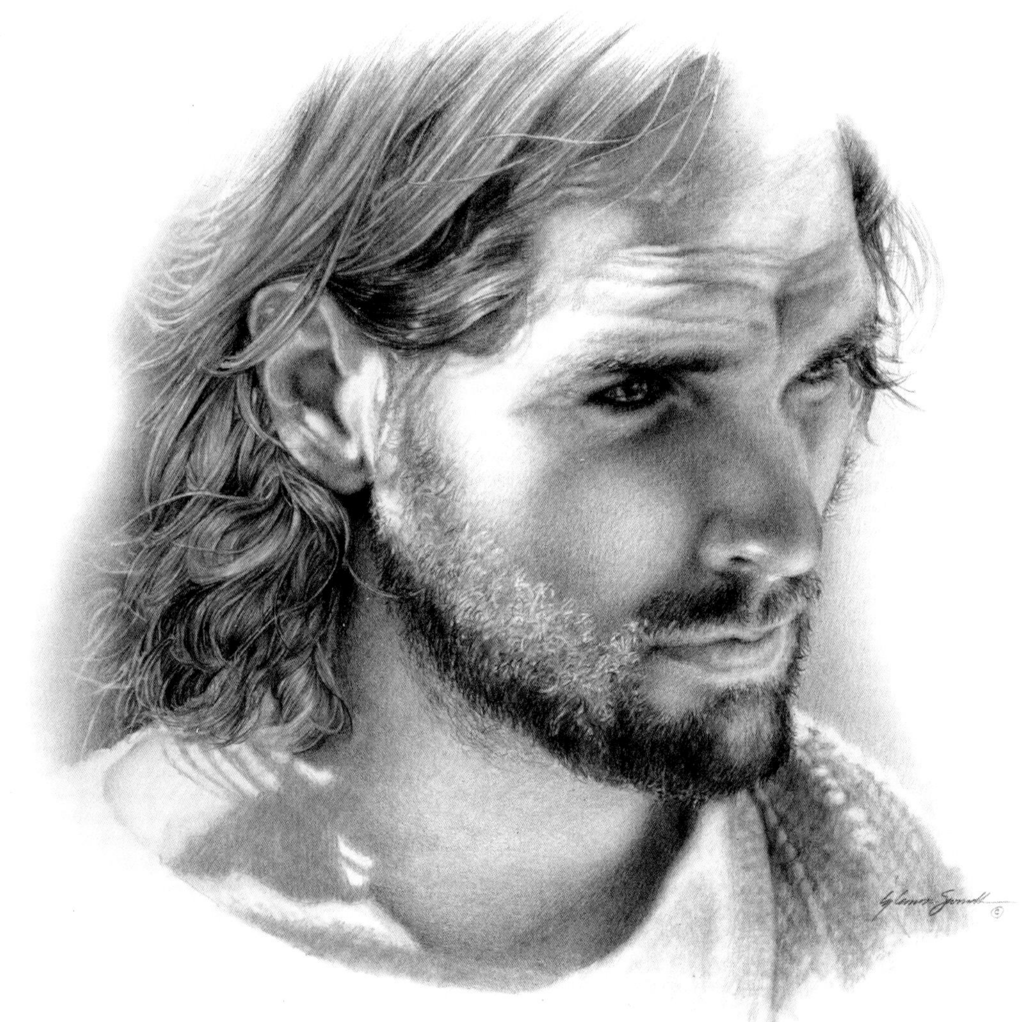

Come Follow Me

The Teachings of Jesus

by Liz Lemon Swindle

Learn of Me

Early in His ministry, Jesus sat on the shores of Galilee and said to the multitudes,

" Come unto me, all ye that labour and are heavy laden, and I will give you rest. Take my yoke upon you, and learn of me; for I am meek and lowly in heart: and ye shall find rest unto your souls."

- Matthew 11:28-29

It is only as we walk with Him that we come to learn who He is and how much He loves us. Although our burdens are still upon our shoulders, when we walk together with the Lord and let Him carry them, our burdens feel lighter and, we find the rest He so freely gives.

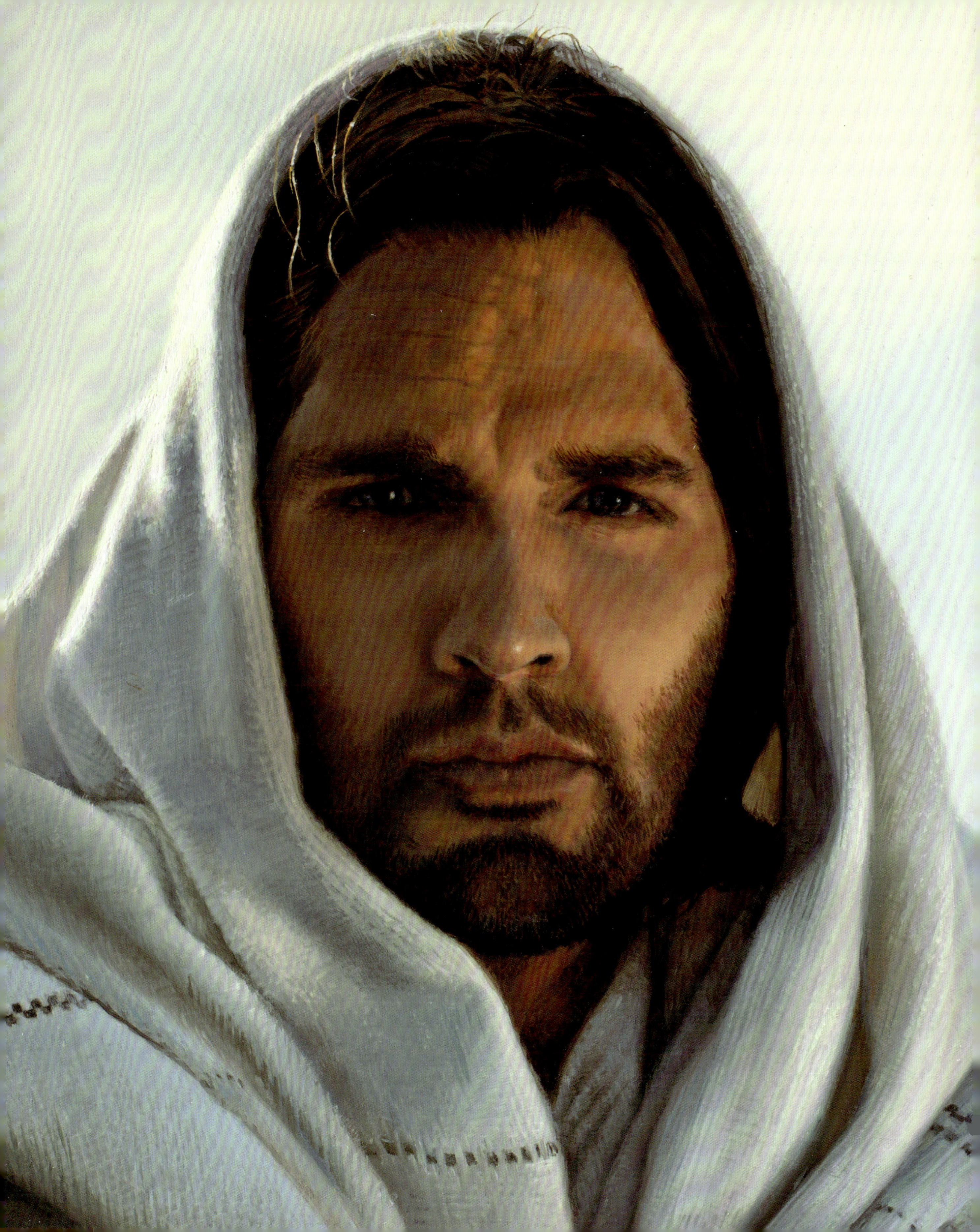

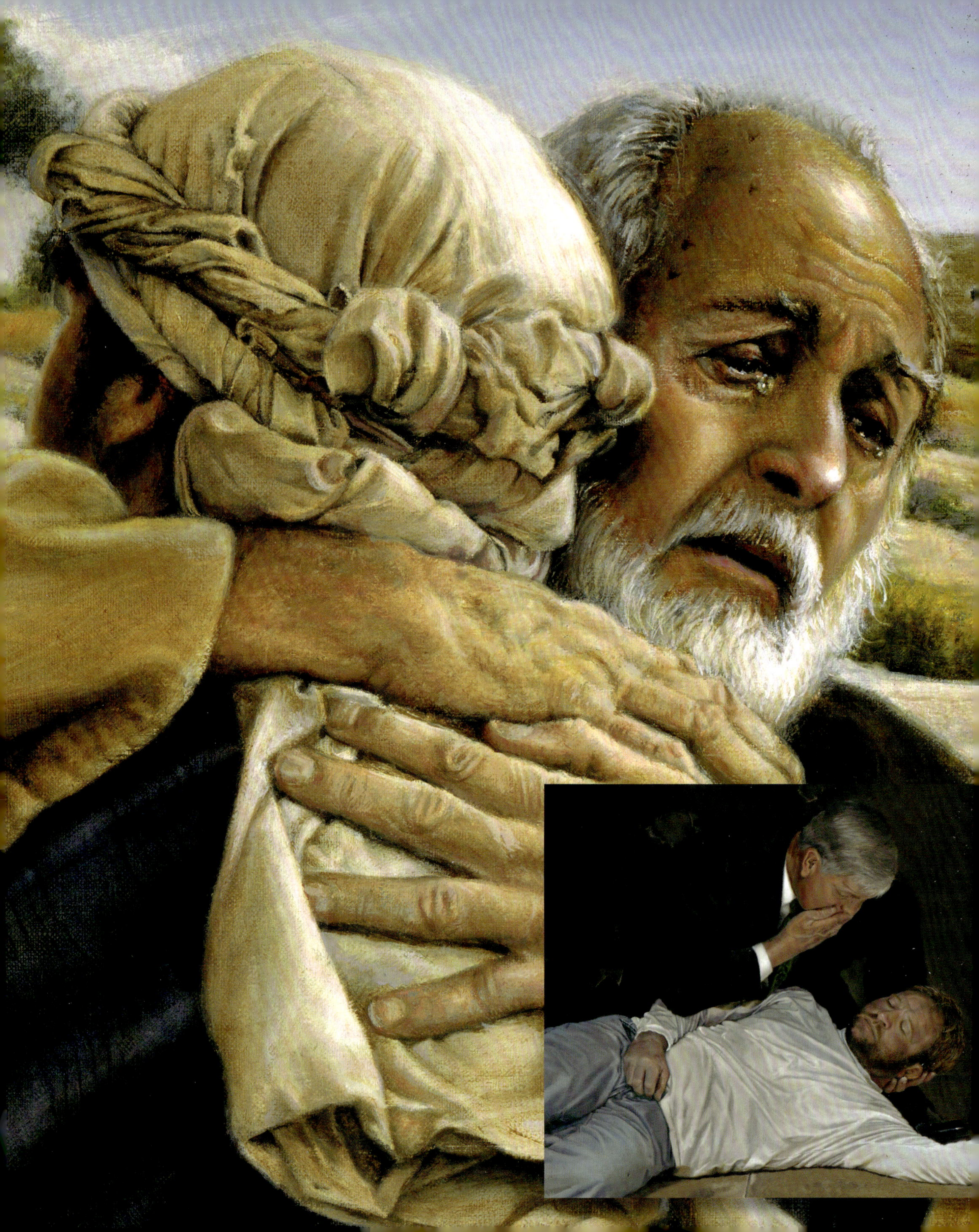

Return

A father had two sons. The younger left home taking his inheritance and spending it foolishly. When this prodigal son realized his situation, he determined to return to his father and ask to be just a hired servant. The father, took him back not as a servant, but as his son.

"Bring forth the best robe, and put it on him; and put a ring on his hand, and shoes on his feet: And bring hither the fatted calf, and kill it; and let us eat, and be merry: For this my son was dead, and is alive again; he was lost, and is found."

- Luke 15:22-24

What parent has not spent countless nights on their knees pleading for their children? And what parent has not looked to the "horizon" hoping to catch a glimpse of a son or daughter that isn't there.

This painting is the hope of every parent. The hope that each of us will one day find our children safely in our arms.

To Fulfill All Righteousness

Christ was perfect and did not need baptism for forgiveness of sins. Yet, the Father commanded that at all men must be baptized to enter the Kingdom of Heaven. In perfect humility, Christ submitted to the will of the Father and was baptized by immersion.

"And lo a voice from heaven, saying, This is my beloved Son, in whom I am well pleased."

\- Matthew 3:17

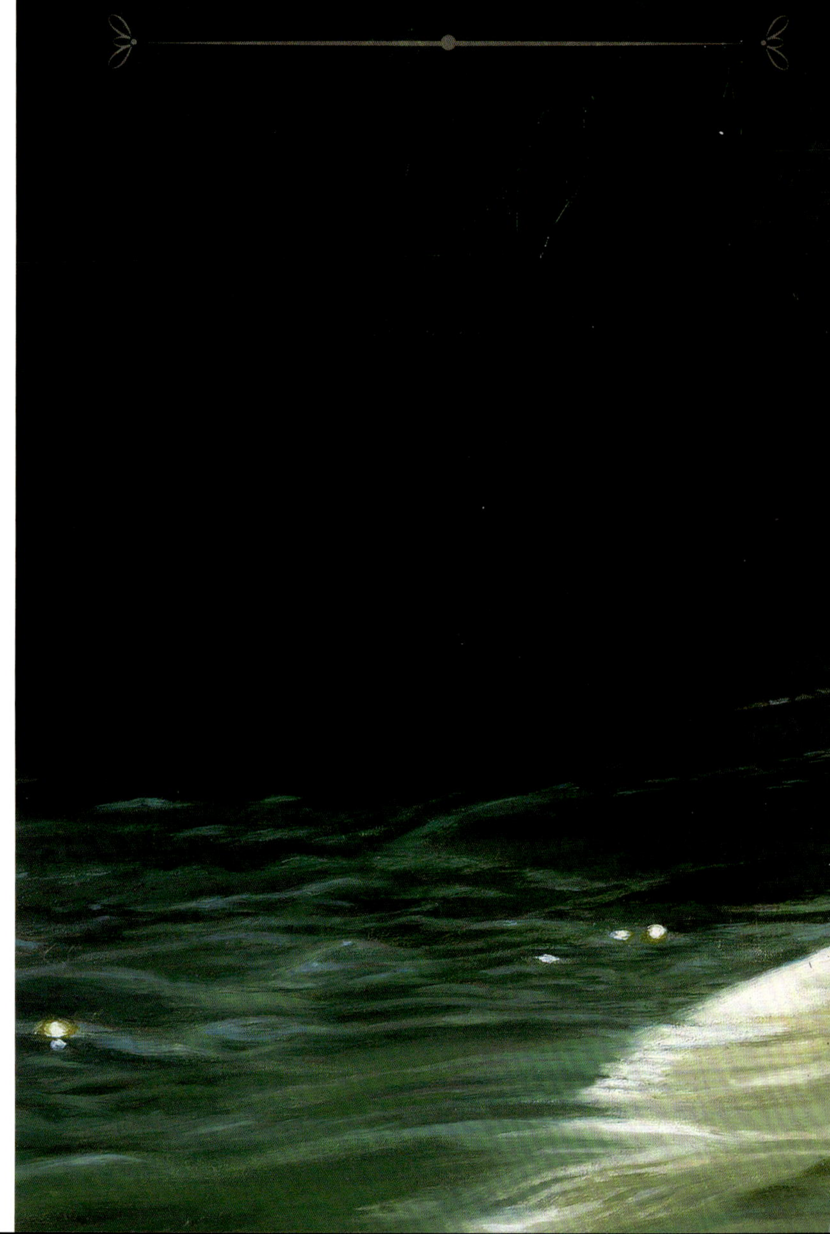

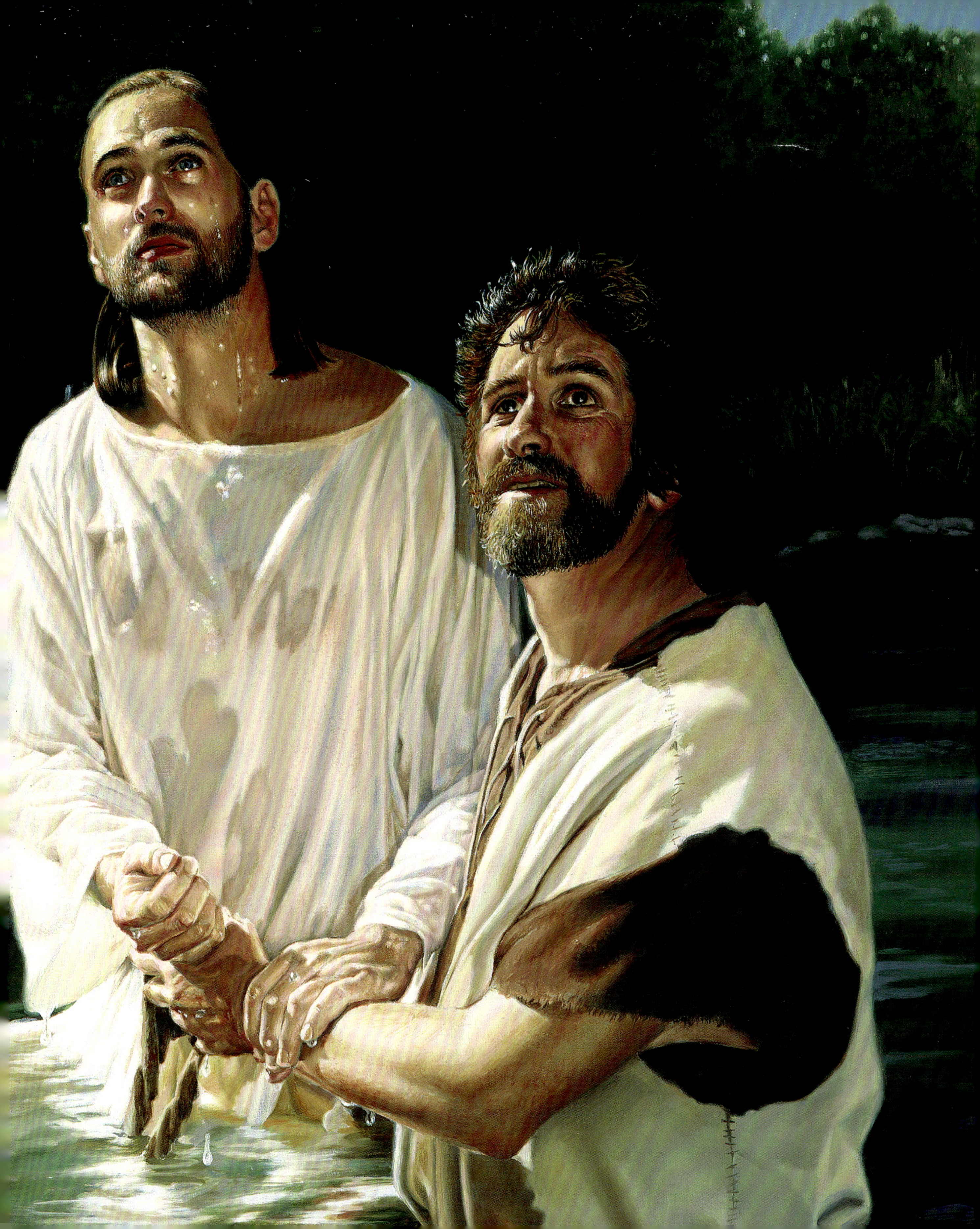

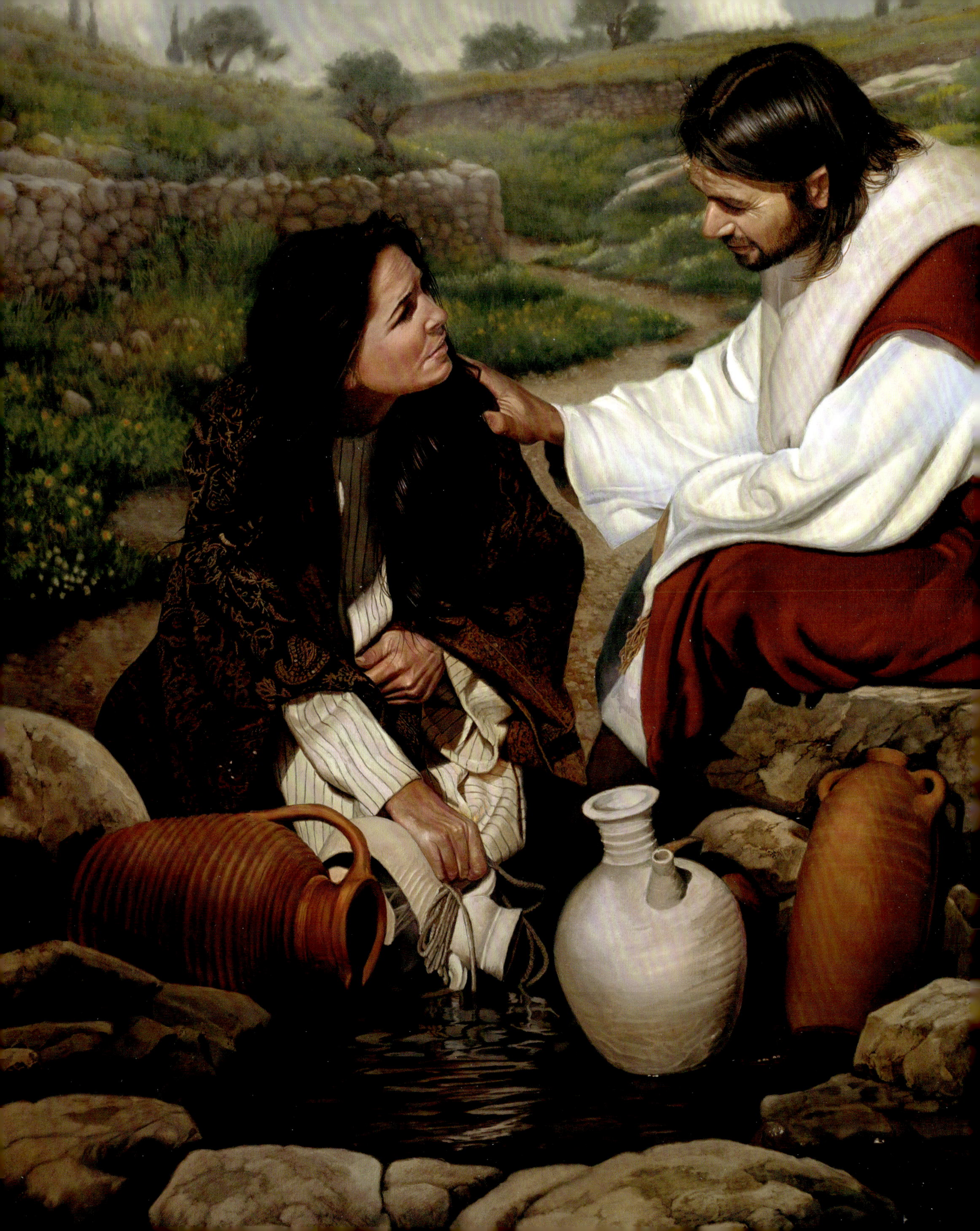

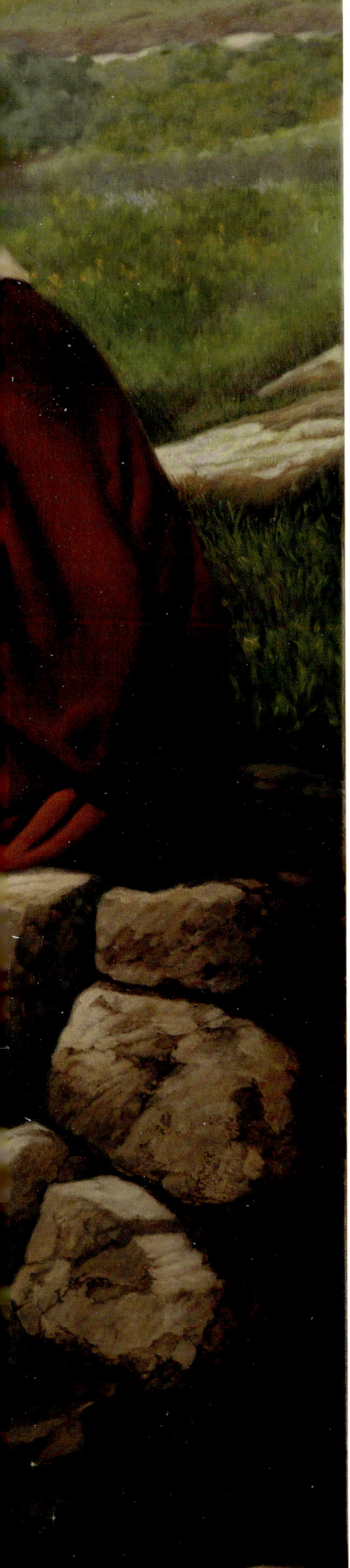

Woman at the Well

A woman came to a well to draw water. There she found the Savior resting from a long journey. She was surprised when He asked for a drink because she was a Samaritan, a group despised by the Jews. She said, *"How is it that thou, being a Jew, asketh drink of me... for the Jews have no dealings with the Samaritans."* (John 4:9)

"But whosoever drinketh of the water that I shall give him shall never thirst; but the water that I shall give him shall be in him a well of water springing up into everlasting life."

- John 4:14

We often feel like this woman, and judge ourselves unworthy to be with the Lord. As we go forward in faith, we come to find, as the woman did, that Jesus knows us each personally. He does not see us as unworthy, but He loves us just as we are with all our flaws and failures.

The Good Samaritan

A lawyer asked Jesus what he should do to inherit eternal life. Jesus replied, *"Thou shalt love the Lord thy God with all thy heart... and thy neighbor as thyself."* The lawyer, then asked, *"Who is my neighbor?"* *(Luke 10:27,29)*

Jesus answered with the parable of the Good Samaritan in which a man was beaten by thieves and left for dead. Both a priest and a Levite passed by the wounded man. Only a despised Samaritan had compassion on him and bound up his wounds and carried him to an inn.

Jesus then asked the lawyer, *"Which now of these three, thinkest thou, was neighbour unto him that fell among the thieves?*

And he said, He that shewed mercy on him. Then said Jesus unto him, Go, and do thou likewise. *(Luke 10:36-37)*

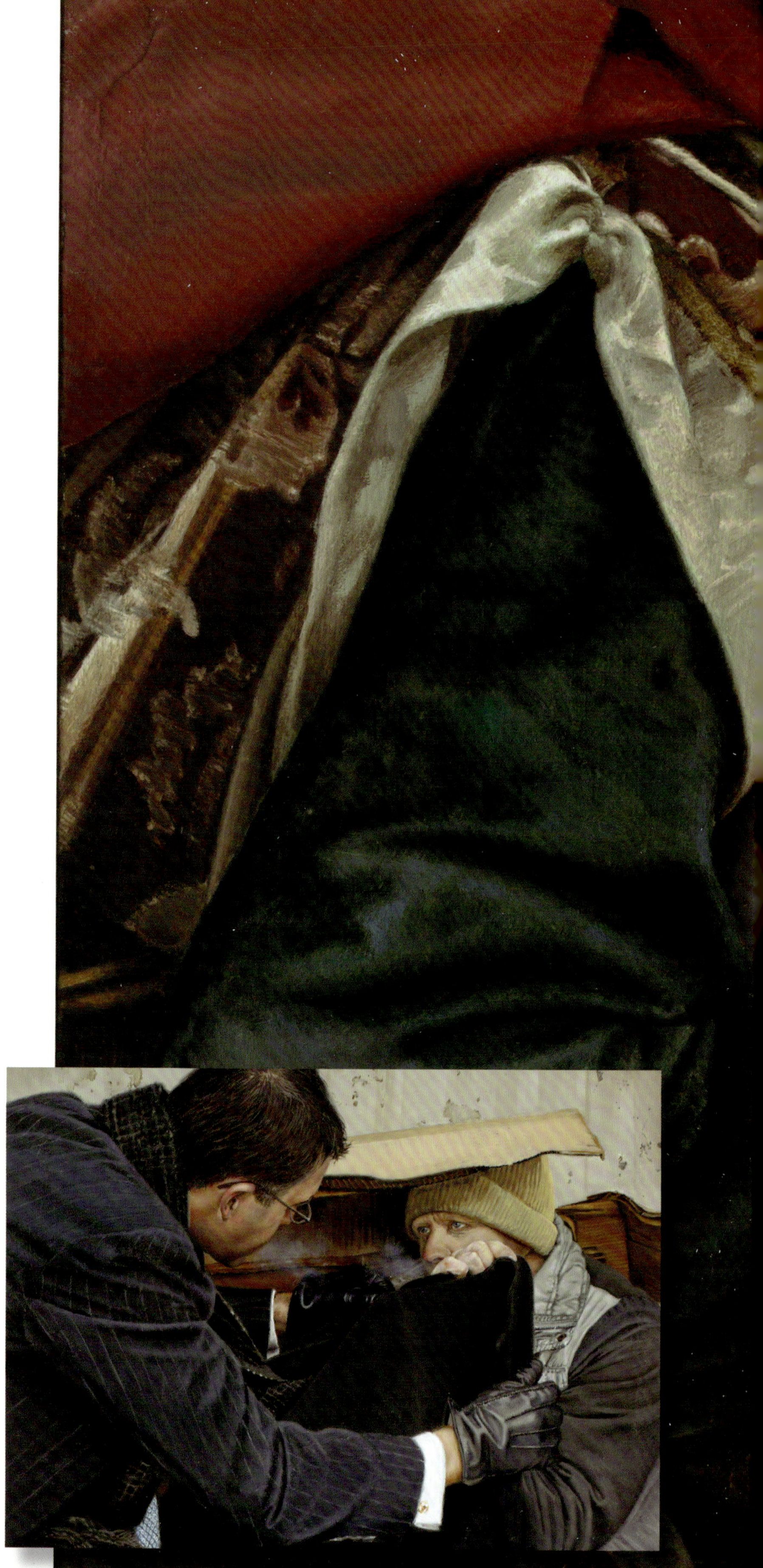

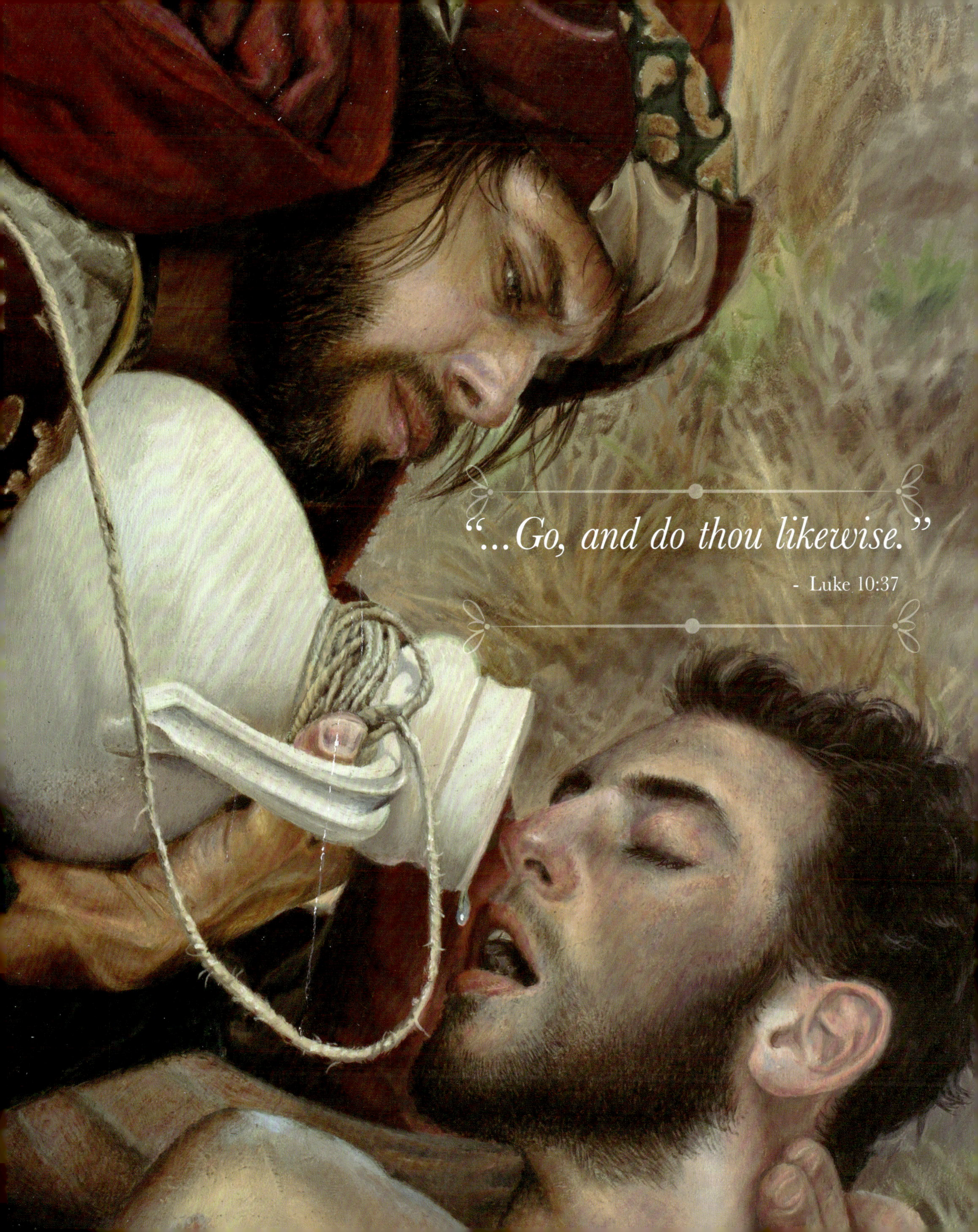
"...Go, and do thou likewise."
- Luke 10:37

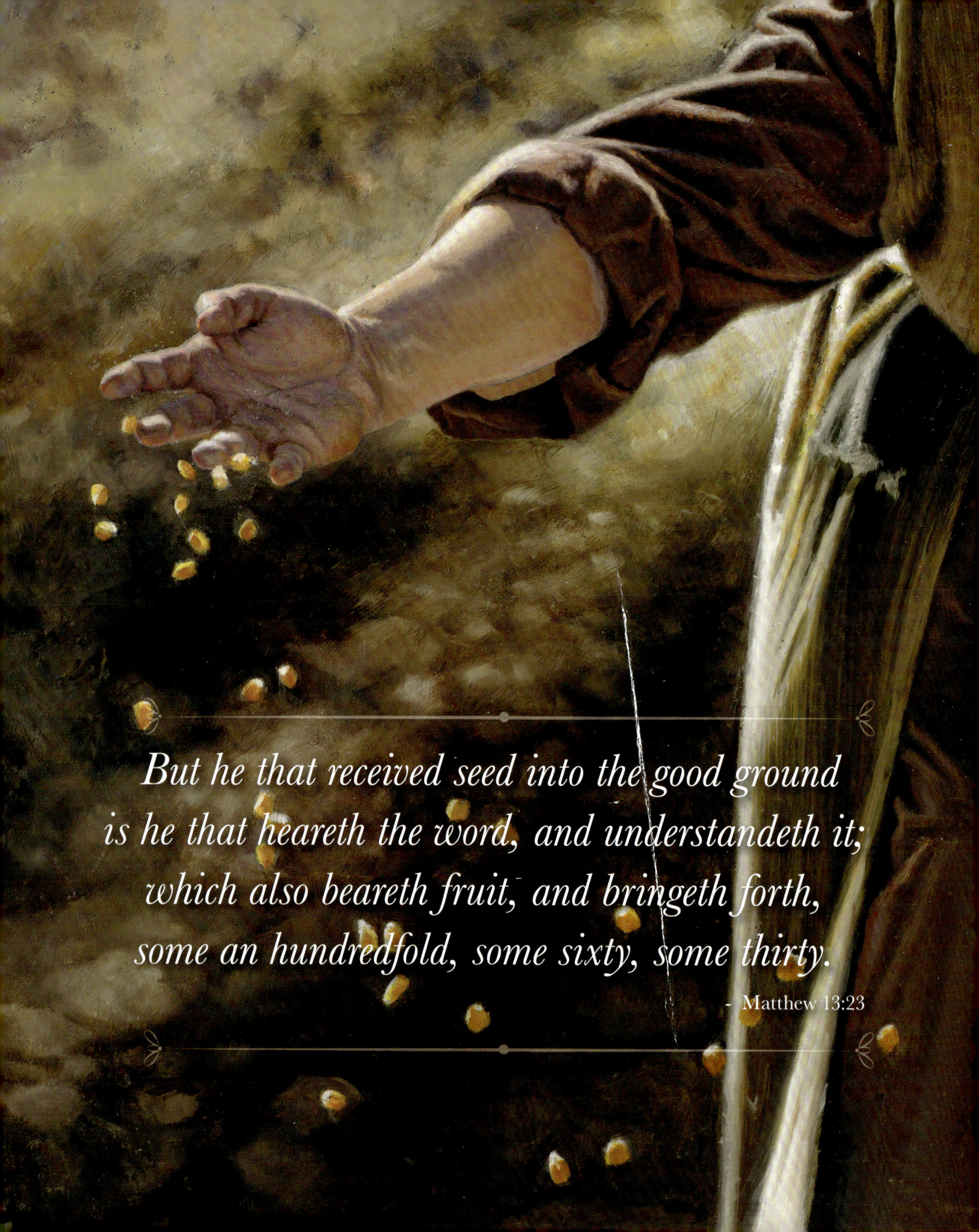
But he that received seed into the good ground
is he that heareth the word, and understandeth it;
which also beareth fruit, and bringeth forth,
some an hundredfold, some sixty, some thirty.
- Matthew 13:23

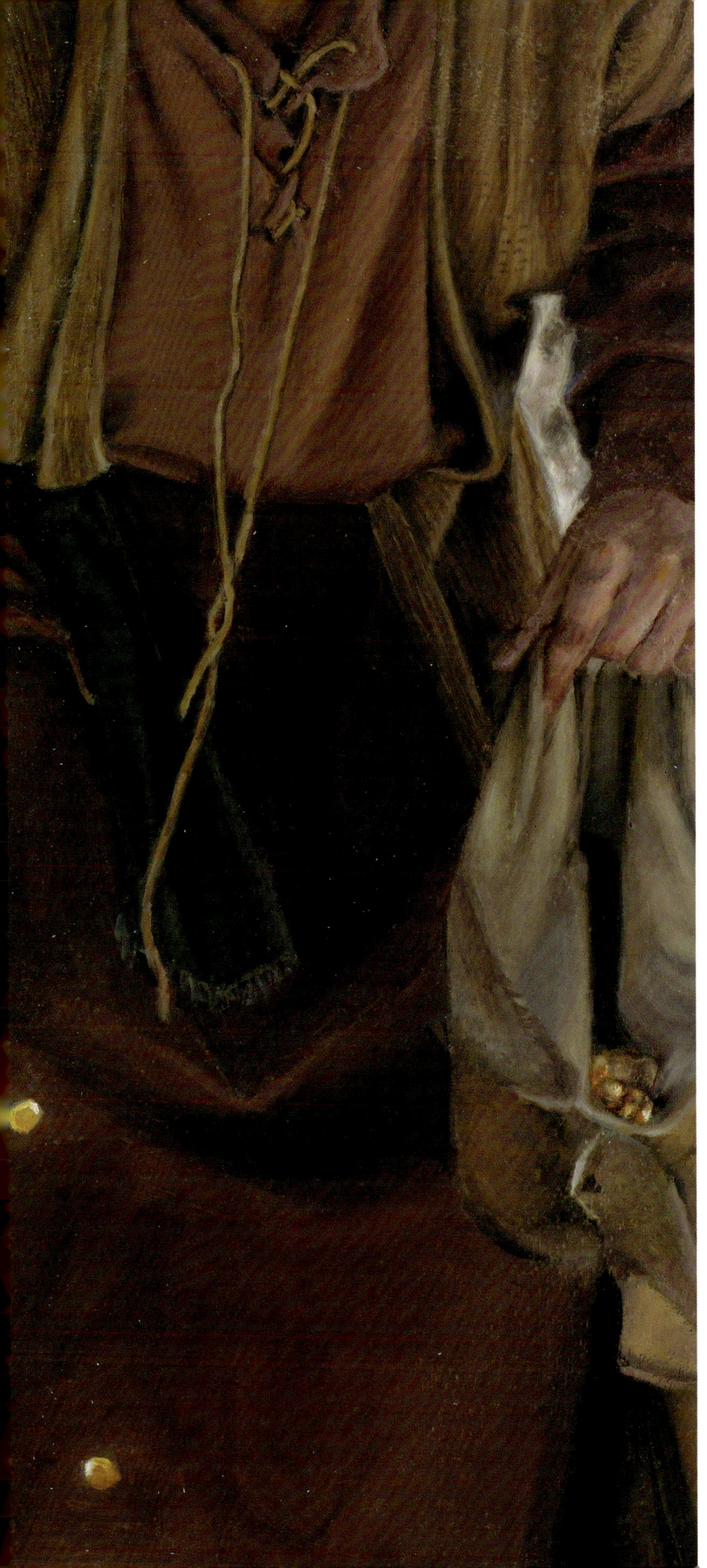

Sower

In the parable of the sower, a man scatters seeds in a field.

The Lord compares the seeds to the Word of God and the ground to the hearts of those who hear the word.

Some have thorny hearts and let their own pleasures and cares choke out the Word of God. Still others have stony hearts and though they give the word a chance, when the heat of persecution shines upon them they give up, and the word is lost.

Finally, some have fertile hearts and make room for the word of God. These bring forth fruit through their actions and become what the Lord wants them to be.

Against the Wind

When Peter saw the Savior walking on the water he asked, *"Lord... bid me come unto thee."* Jesus replied simply, *"Come."* Filled with faith, Peter stepped from the safety of the boat out onto the stormy sea, but as the winds picked up and the waves grew stronger and Peter's faith turned to fear. As he began to sink, He cried, *"Lord, save me."* (Matthew 14:28-30)

And immediately Jesus stretched forth his hand, and caught him, and said unto him, O thou of little faith, wherefore didst thou doubt?

- Matthew 14: 31

Two thousand years later, Christ is still calling to us. As we step from the safety of self-reliance on to the stormy seas of discipleship, we too pray, *"Lord, save me."* With perfect calmness Jesus stills the winds of our doubt, reaches down from heaven and saves us."

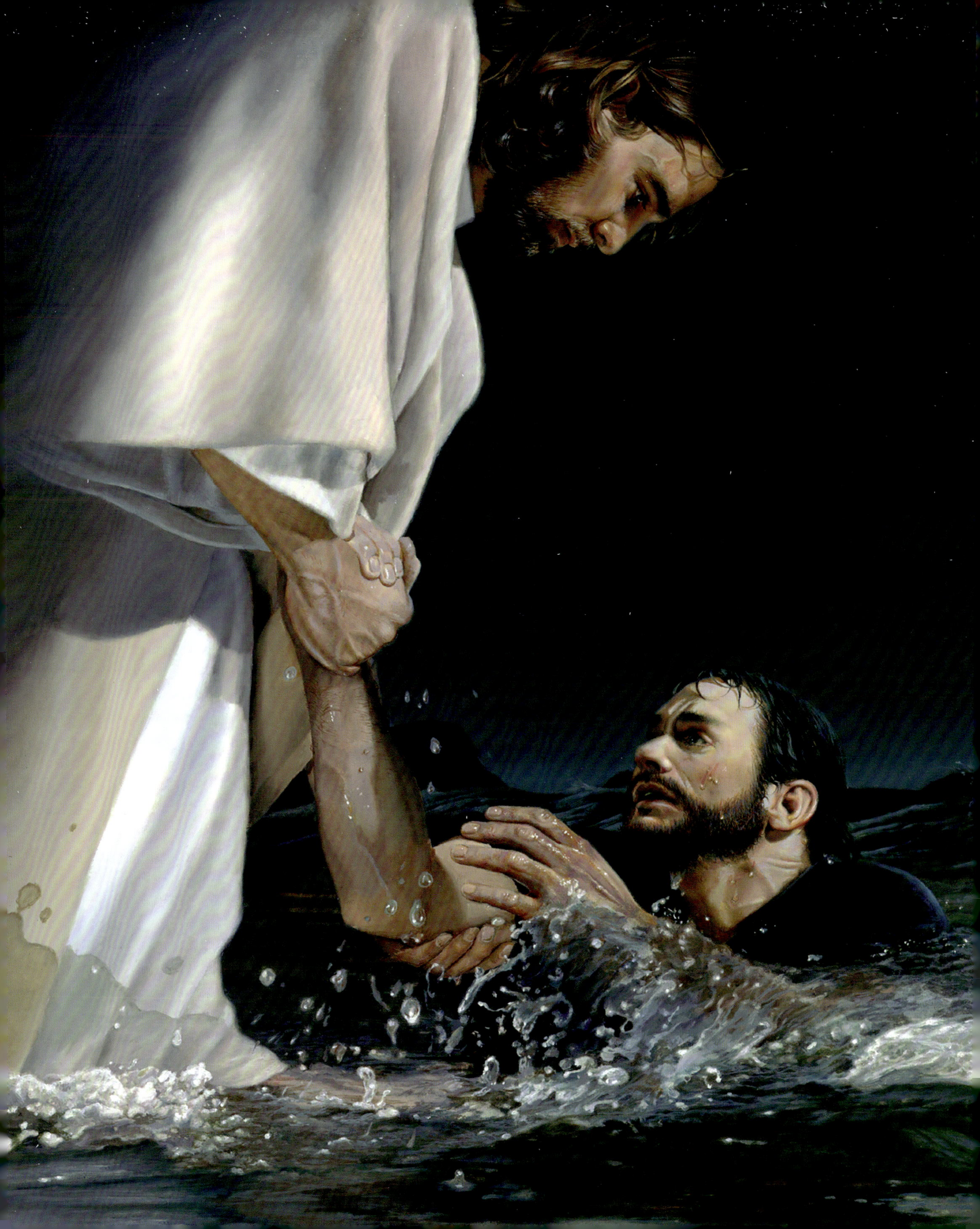

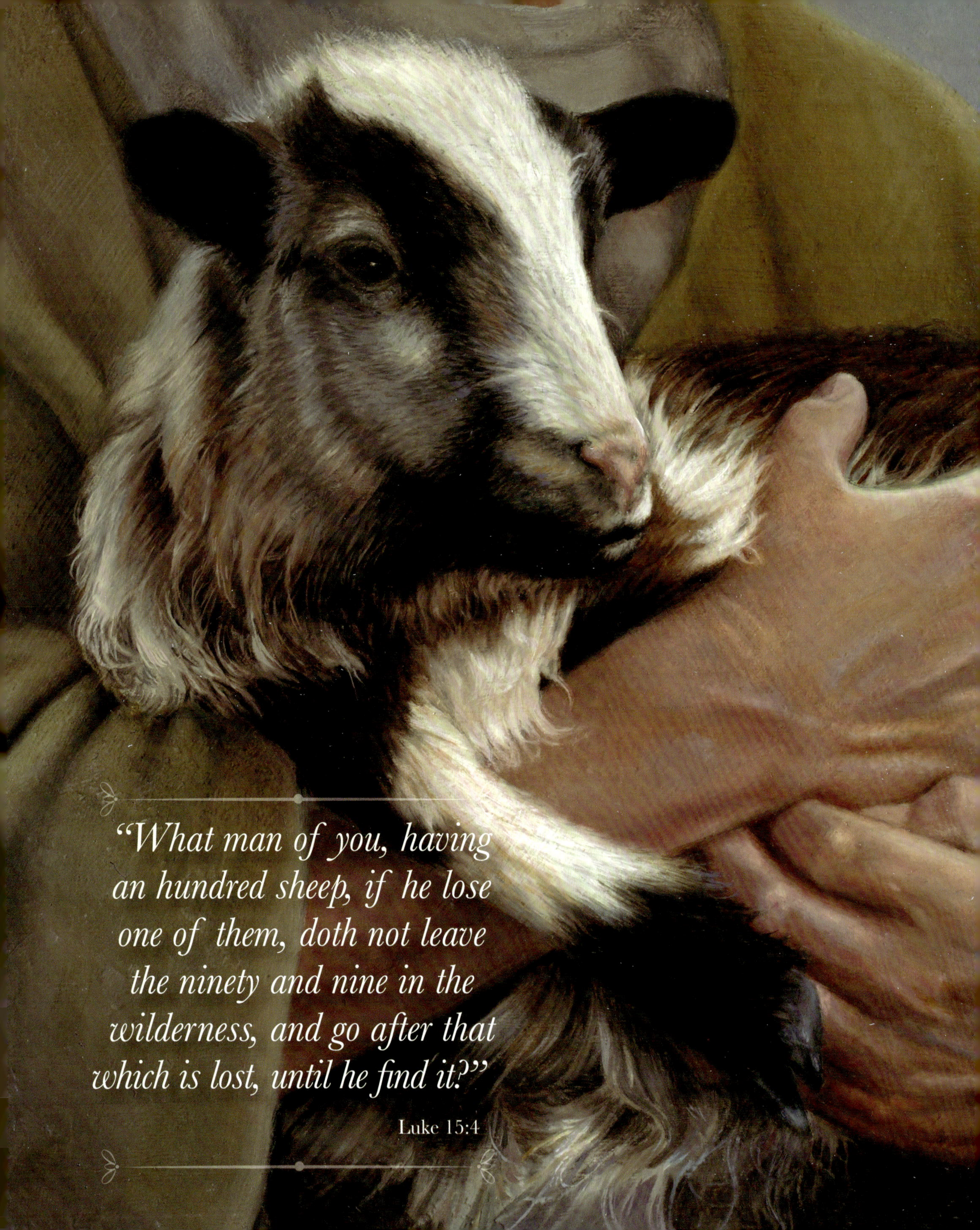
"What man of you, having
an hundred sheep, if he lose
one of them, doth not leave
the ninety and nine in the
wilderness, and go after that
which is lost, until he find it?"
Luke 15:4

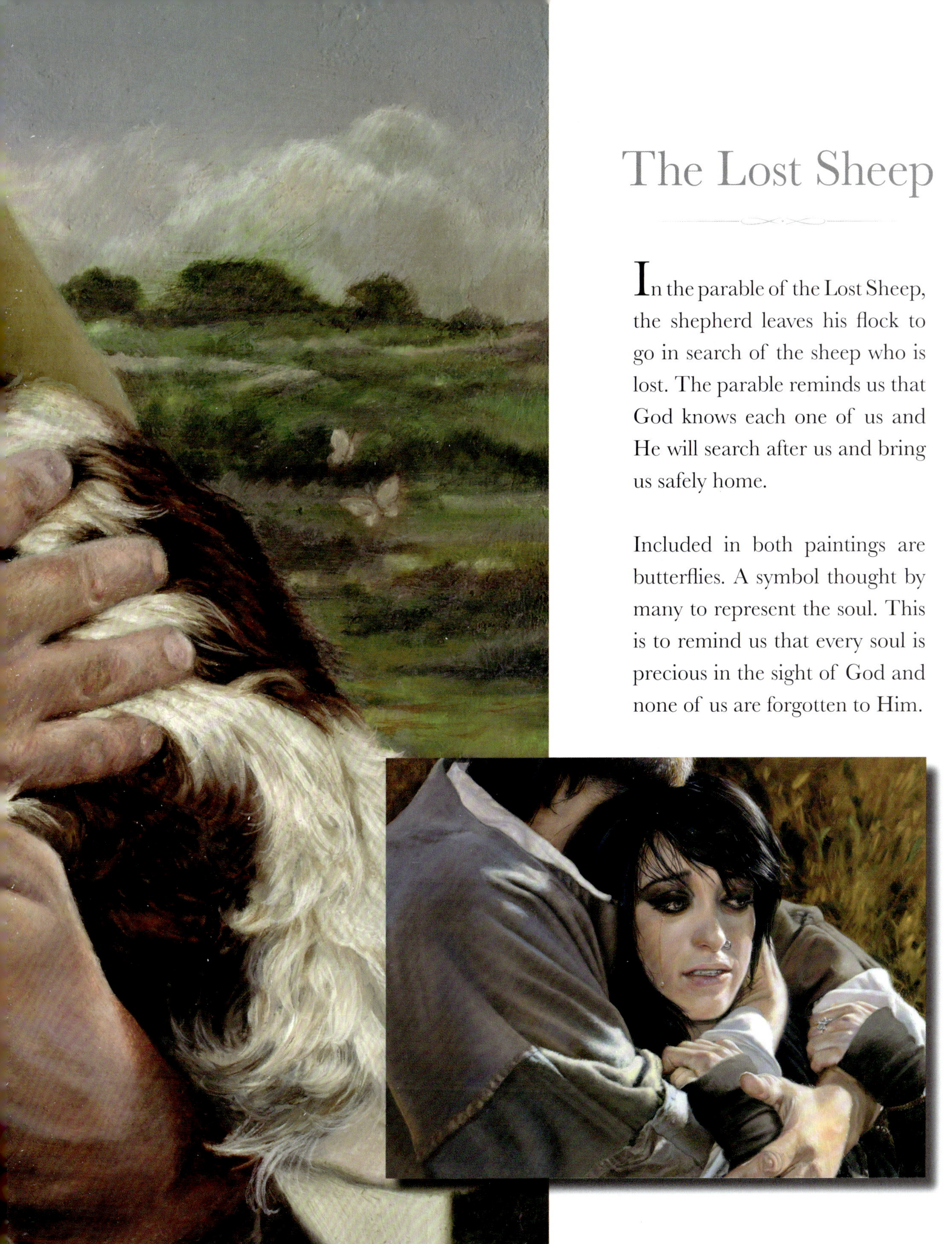

The Lost Sheep

In the parable of the Lost Sheep, the shepherd leaves his flock to go in search of the sheep who is lost. The parable reminds us that God knows each one of us and He will search after us and bring us safely home.

Included in both paintings are butterflies. A symbol thought by many to represent the soul. This is to remind us that every soul is precious in the sight of God and none of us are forgotten to Him.

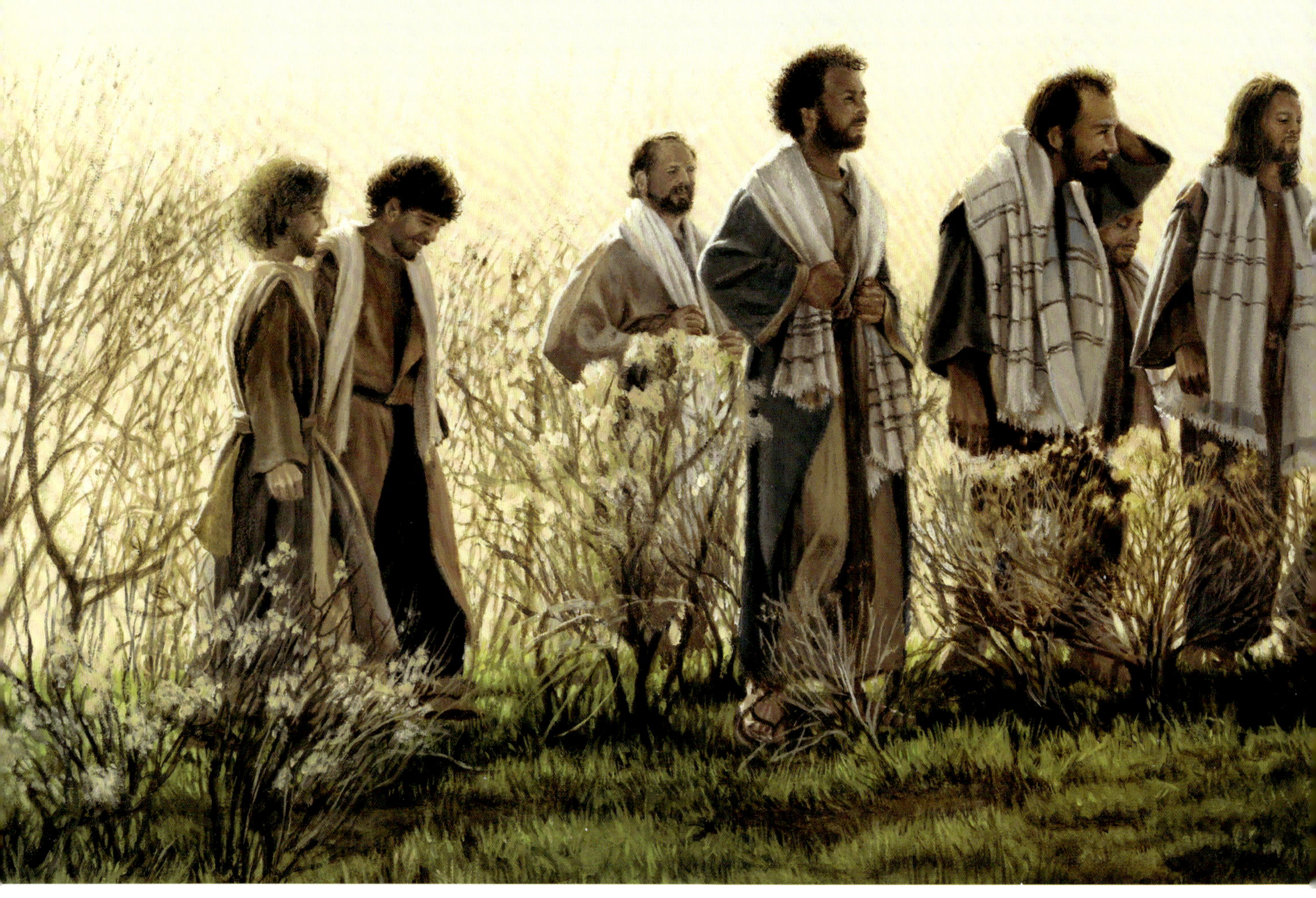

Without Purse or Scrip

Early in His ministry, the Savior called His disciples to go forth and preach his word. These were largely fishermen who must have worried how they would provide for themselves and their families as they left to go and preach. Calming their fears Jesus said, *Provide neither gold, nor silver, nor brass in your purses, ...for the workman is worthy of his meat."* (Matthew 10:9-10)

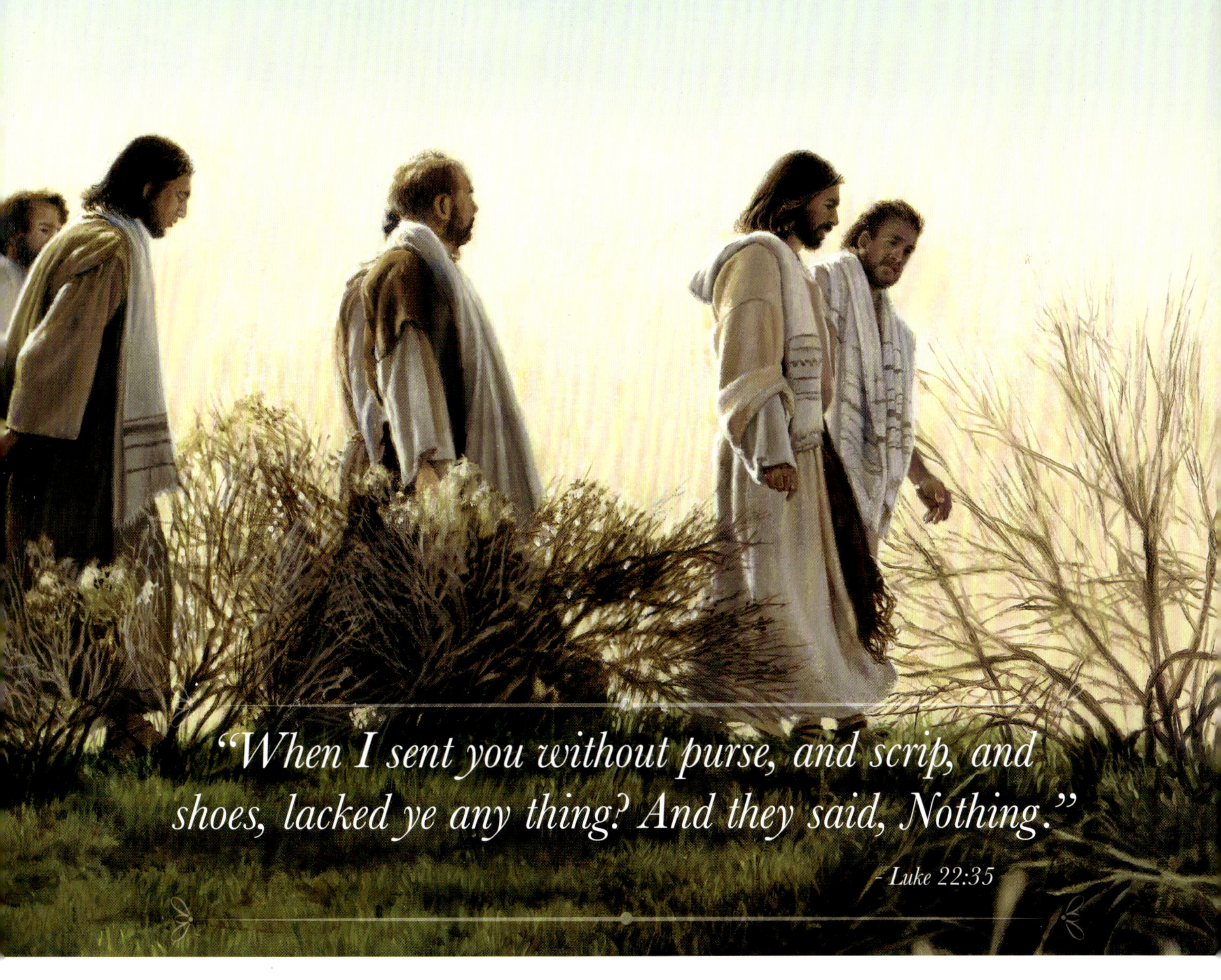

We live in times of great uncertainty when the necessities of life seem harder to come by and where the burden of providing for our families seems heavier than ever. This painting reassures us that although the road may be rough, when we walk with Christ we have everything we need.

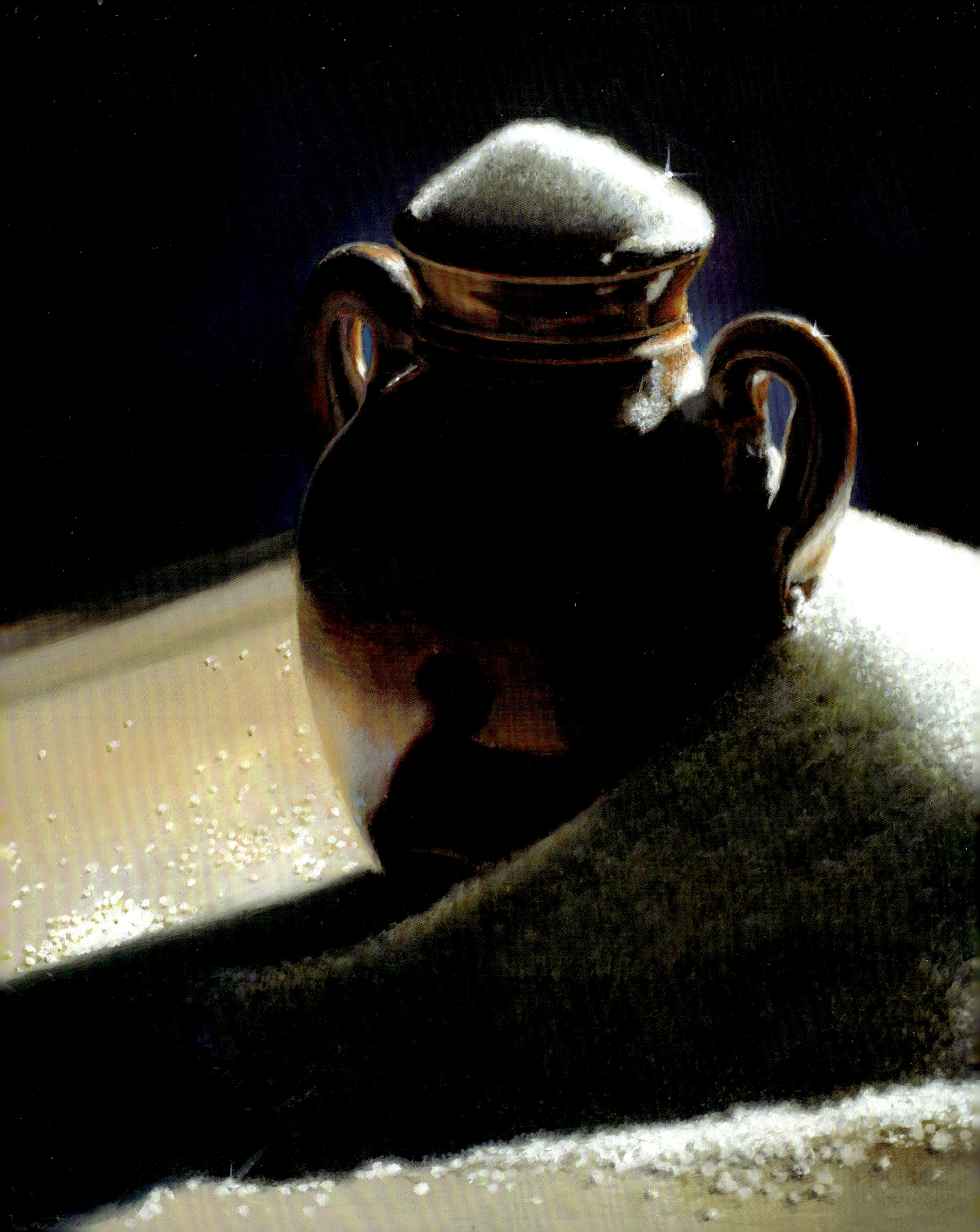

Ye Are the Salt of the Earth

During the sermon on the mount the Lord said;

Ye are the salt of the earth: but if the salt have lost his savour, wherewith shall it be salted? It is thenceforth good for nothing, but to be cast out, and to be trodden under foot of men.

Matthew 5:13

Jesus' disciples understood the cleansing power of salt and the significance it had in adding flavor to life. They understood it's preserving power in a world without refrigerators. They realized that salt loses it's savor when mixed with something else.

All of these symbols were involved in the Savior's parable, but there was one that stands out above the others. Salt was an integral part of temple sacrifices and so became associated with the covenant people. Through this parable Jesus reminds us that we become salt when we make and keep covenants with God. As we remain true to those covenants and avoid mixing with worldly influences, we can be cleansed, preserved, and become the salt of the earth.

As a Hen Gathereth Her Chicks

On the night before Jesus was crucified, He went to the Mount of Olives looking down on Jerusalem, the city and the people He loved, He lamented, "... *how often would I have gathered thy children together, even as a hen gathereth her chickens under her wings, and ye would not!* (Matthew 23:37)

God still longs to gather us under His wing. He is anxious to protect us and provide comfort. He often does this through the love and efforts of others here on earth.

In the painting are twelve chicks, symbolic of the number of Jesus' apostles, those who assisted Him, as a reminder that today we are His hands to gather His children safely home.

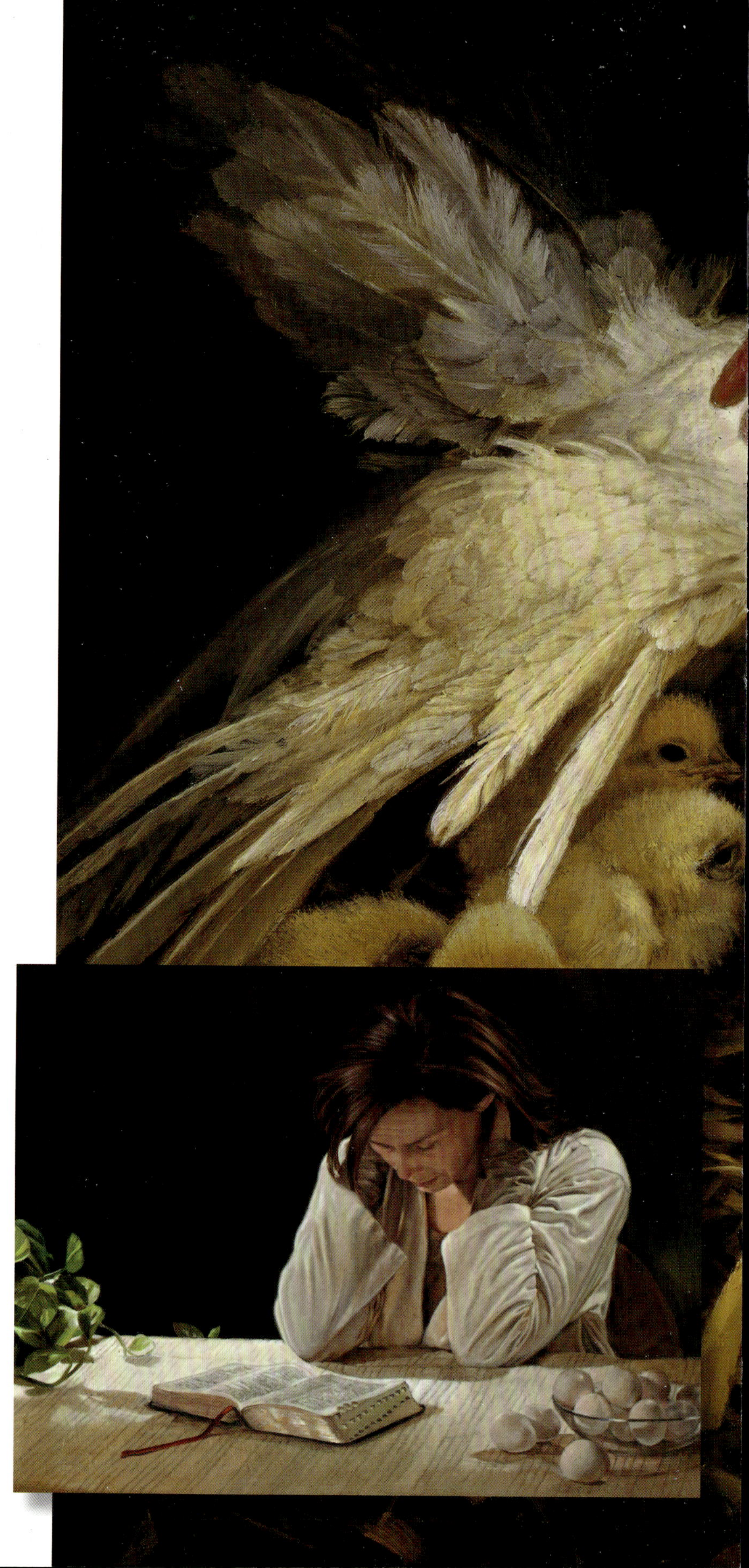

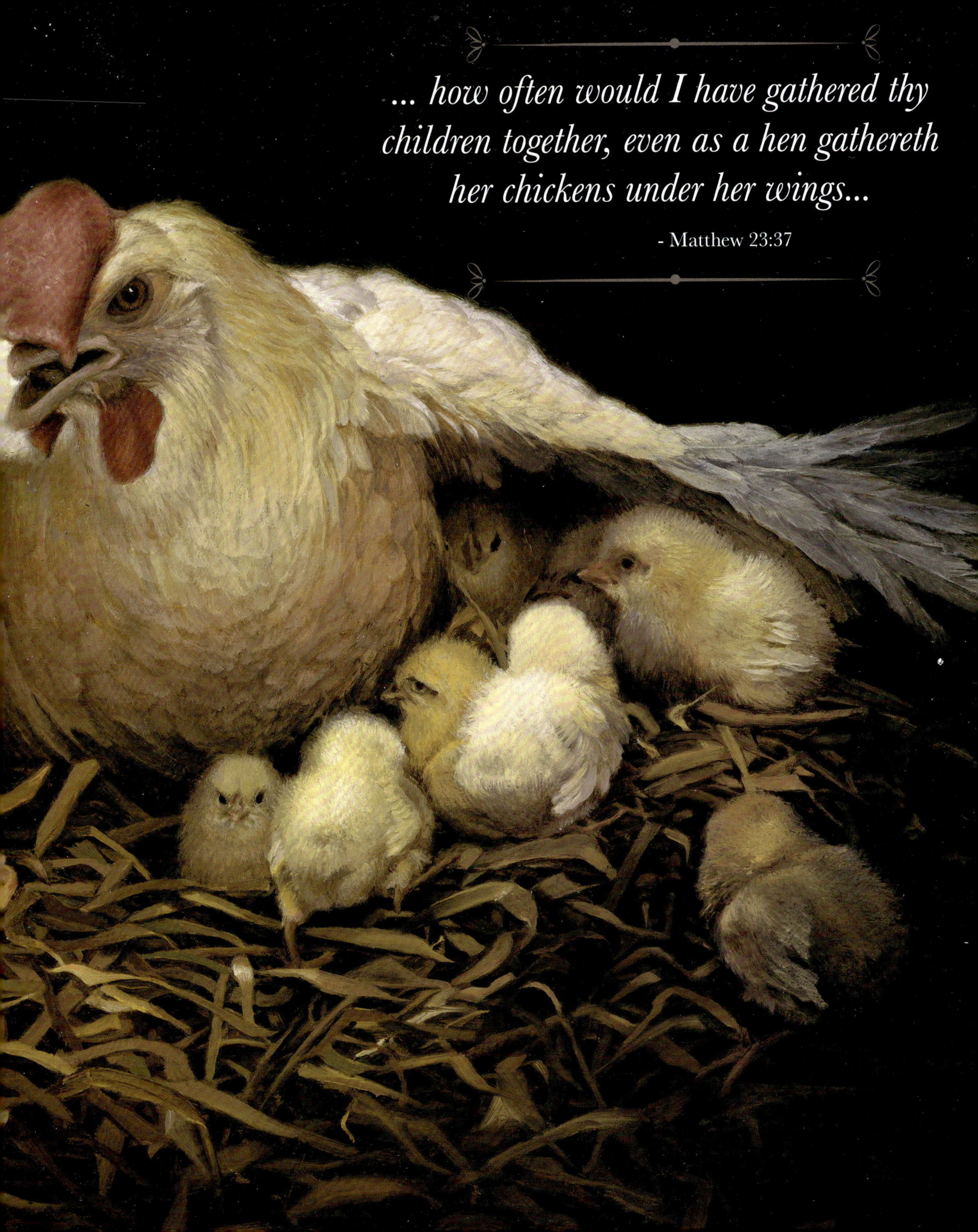
... how often would I have gathered thy children together, even as a hen gathereth her chickens under her wings...
- Matthew 23:37

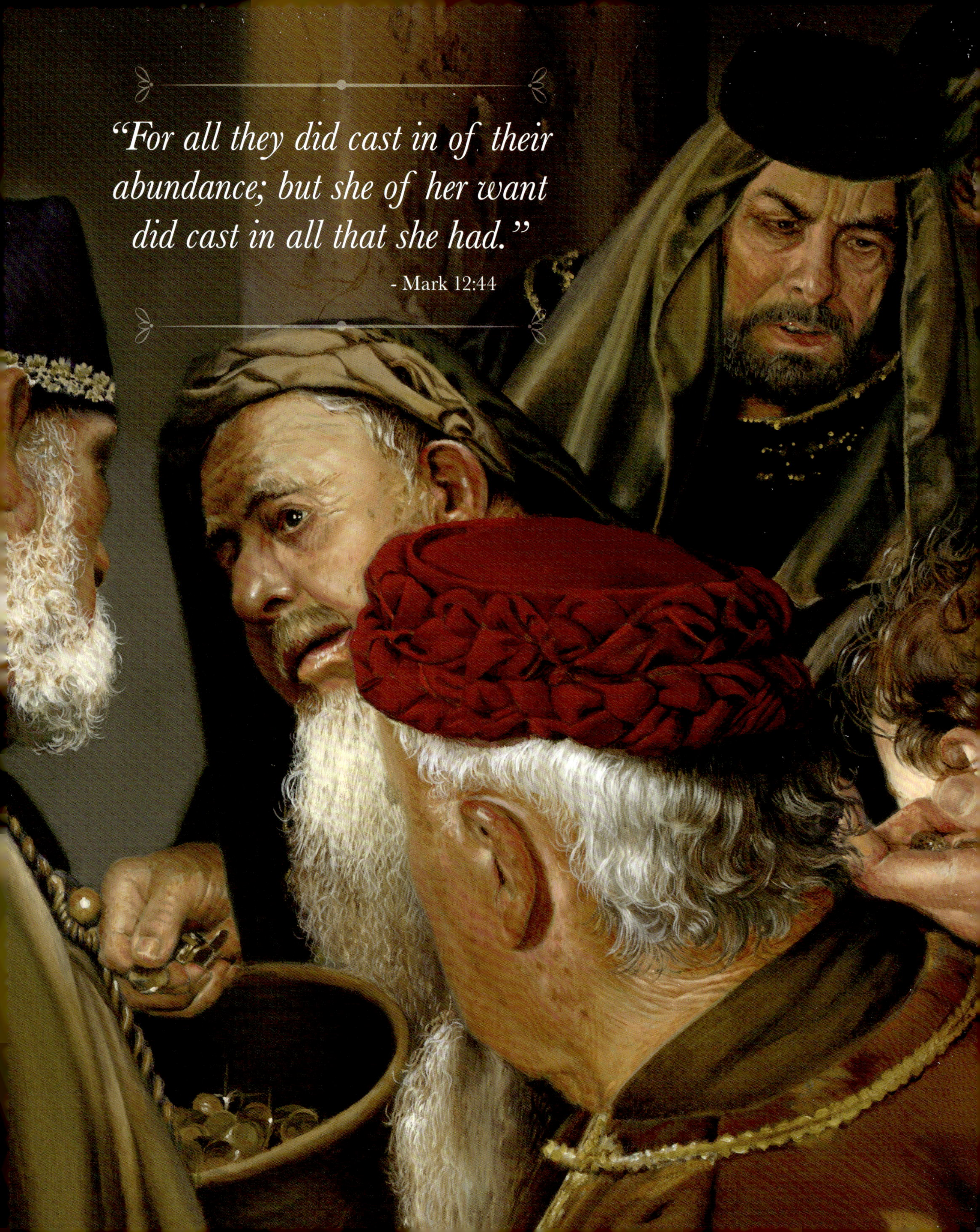
"For all they did cast in of their
abundance; but she of her want
did cast in all that she had."
- Mark 12:44

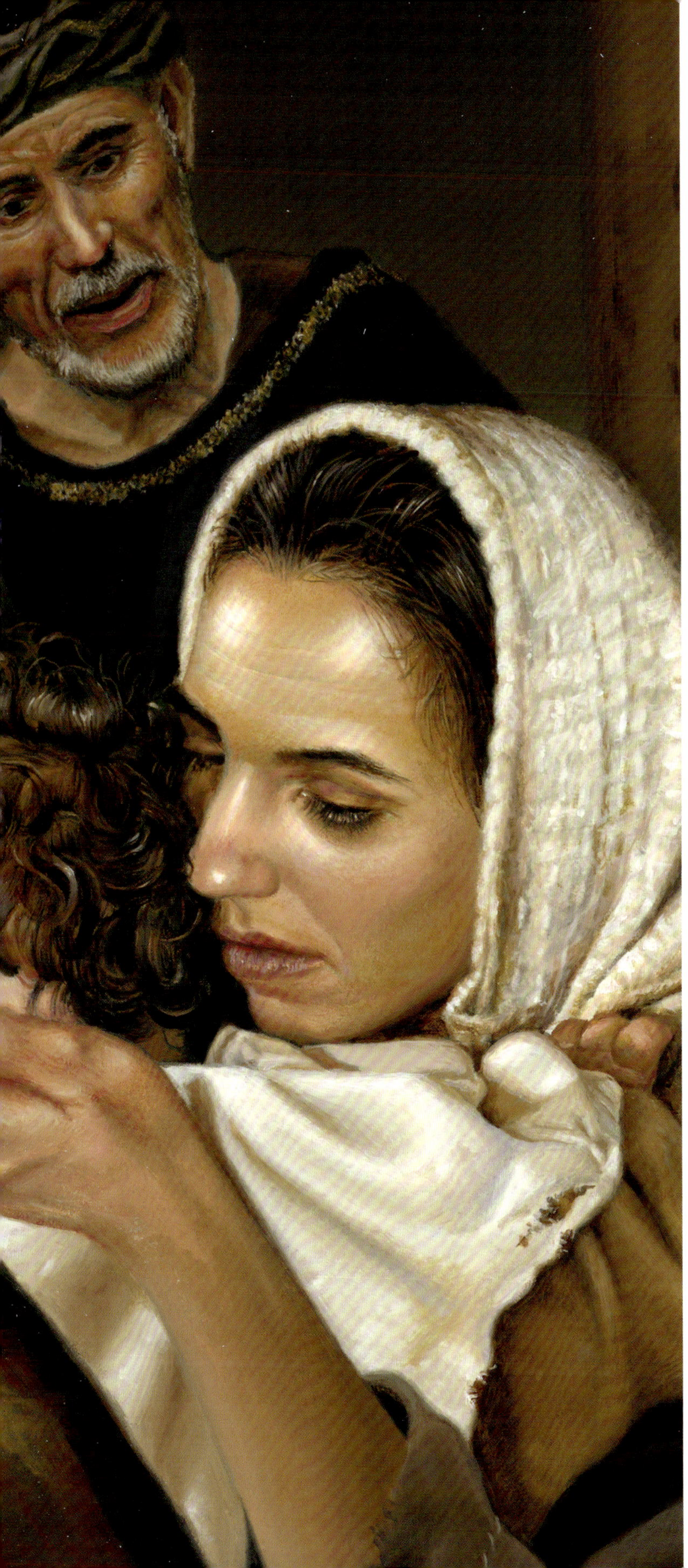

The Widow's Mites

How often have we had to make the widow's choice? In times when there is plenty the choice to give seems easy, but on those days when there isn't enough to go around, the decision to give seems overwhelming, even impossible.

When we can't seem to make ends meet and things are tight, We know that giving is still the proper answer. Throughout our lives when we cast in our "mites", regardless of our circumstances, the Lord always keeps His promises and throws open the windows of heaven.

Let the Children Come

Too often we look on the Savior as distant and removed from us. We remember Him as the God of the Universe possessing all power and might, yet forget that He is our personal Savior.

This piece was created with the idea that any child would be encouraged to think of Him as a friend. And, more importantly, that He would be the first One they could turn to for peace and comfort.

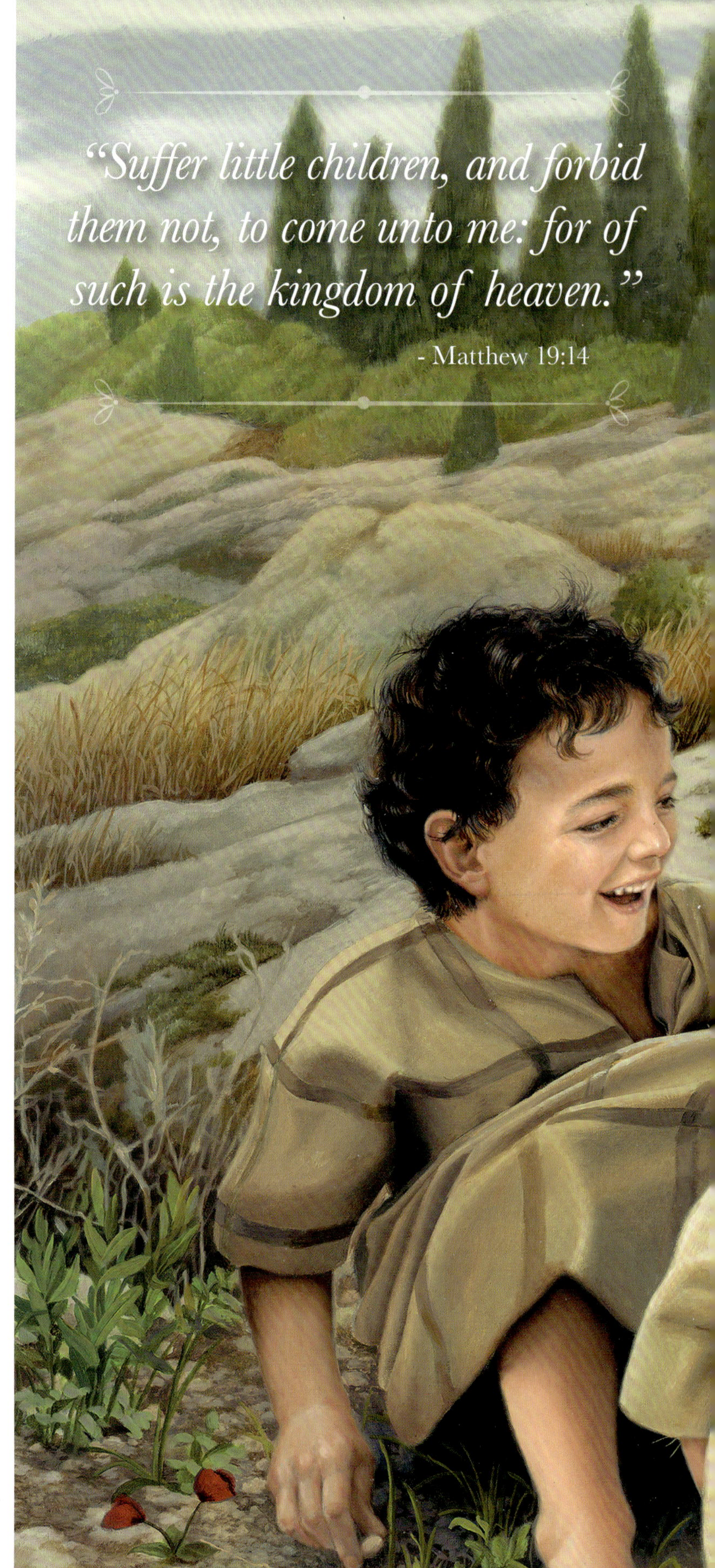

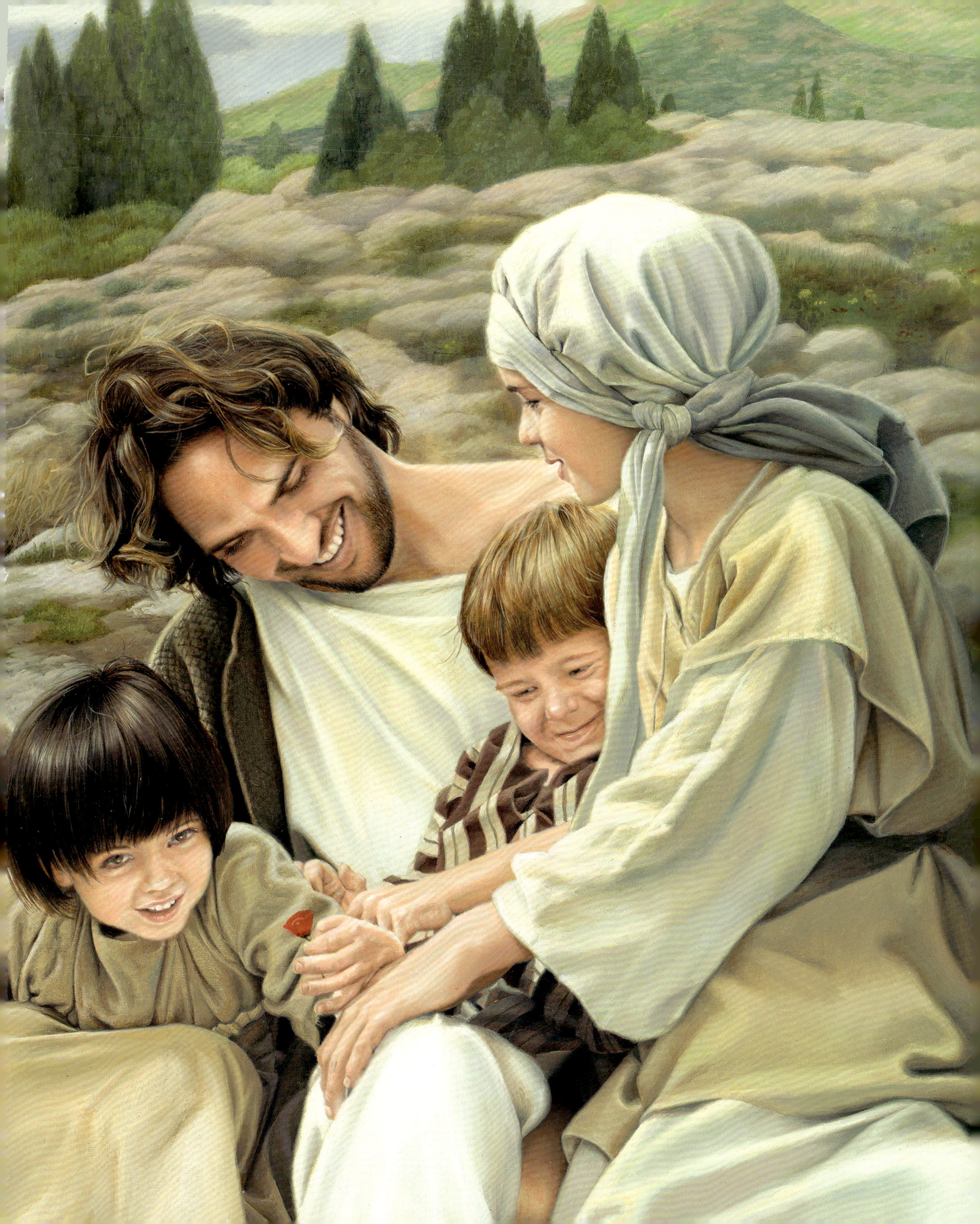

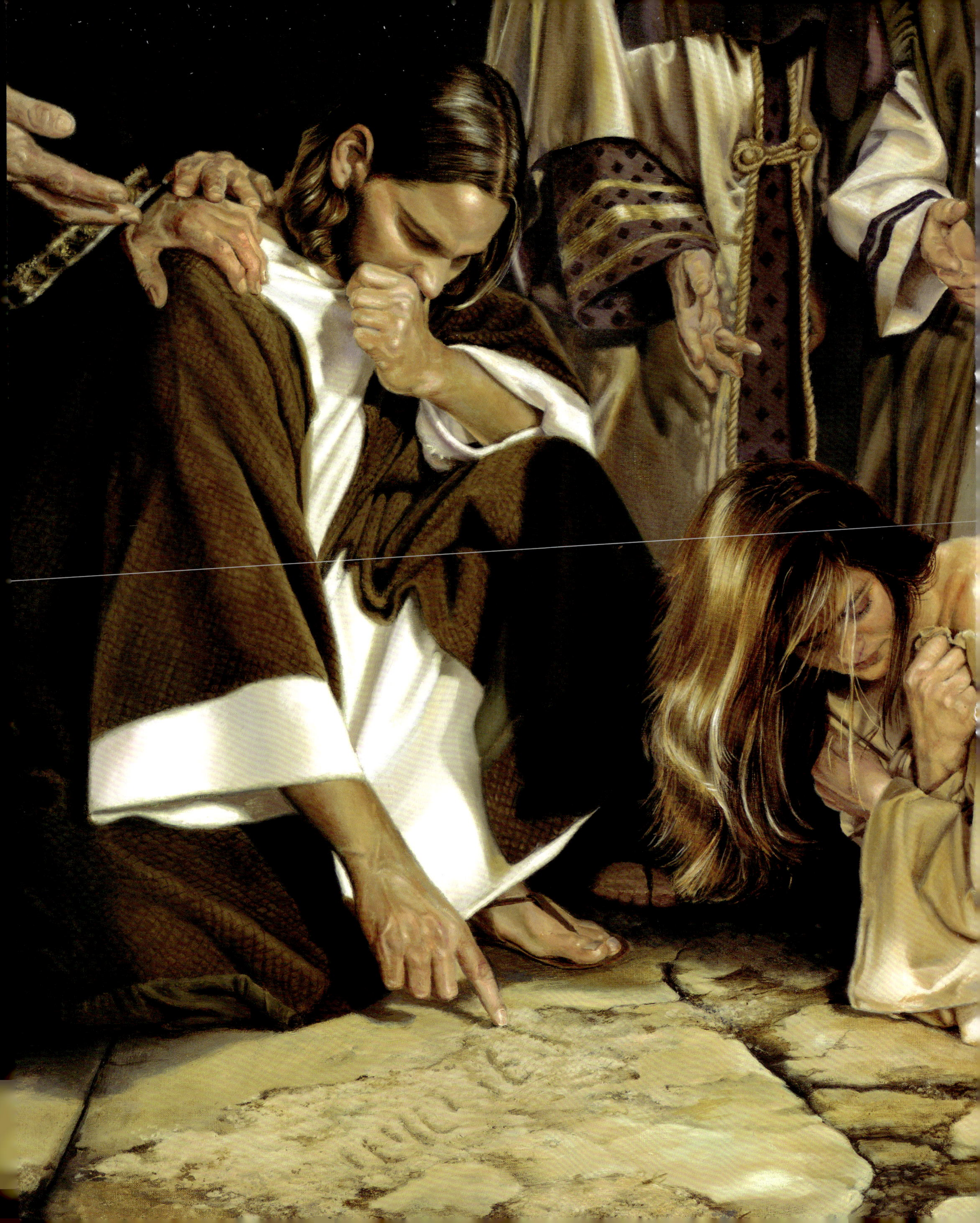

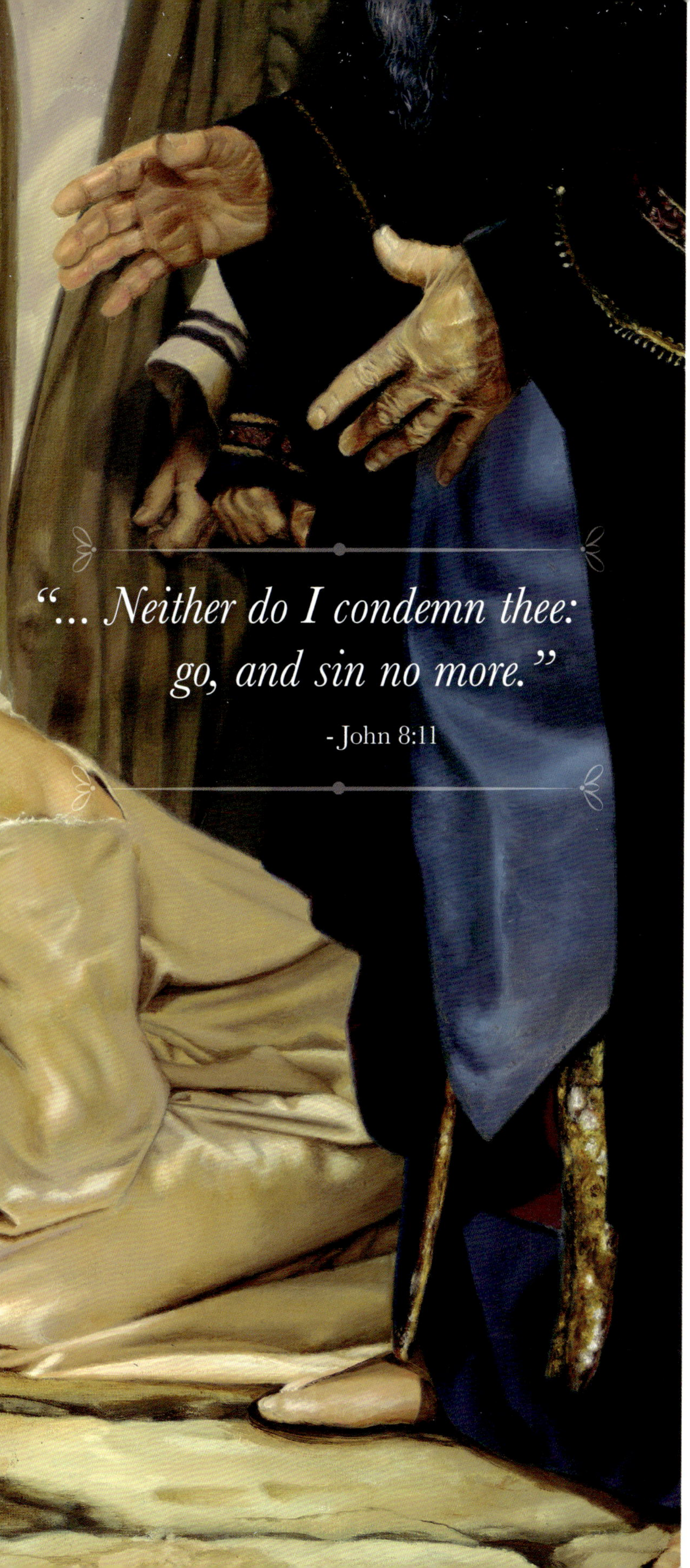

He that is Without Sin

The leaders of the Jews brought an adulterous woman before the Lord asking if she should be stoned. Christ simply said, *"He that is without sin among you, let him first cast a stone at her."* *(John 8:7)*

Convicted by their own conscience, the crowd disappeared leaving only Christ and the accused.

In our lives it's easy for us to focus on condemning the sins of others as opposed to showing mercy to the sinner. It is important to remember this story and the Savior's power to heal and forgive.

Ye Are the Light of the World

When our lives are filled with the joy that comes from following Jesus Christ, our actions become a light in the darkness.

Etched on the side of this lamp are the seven continents, reminding each of us that when we live as Christ taught we truly are *"the light of the world."*

*"Ye are the light of the world.
Let your light so shine before men, that
they may see your good works, and glorify
your Father which is in heaven."*

- Matthew 5:14,16

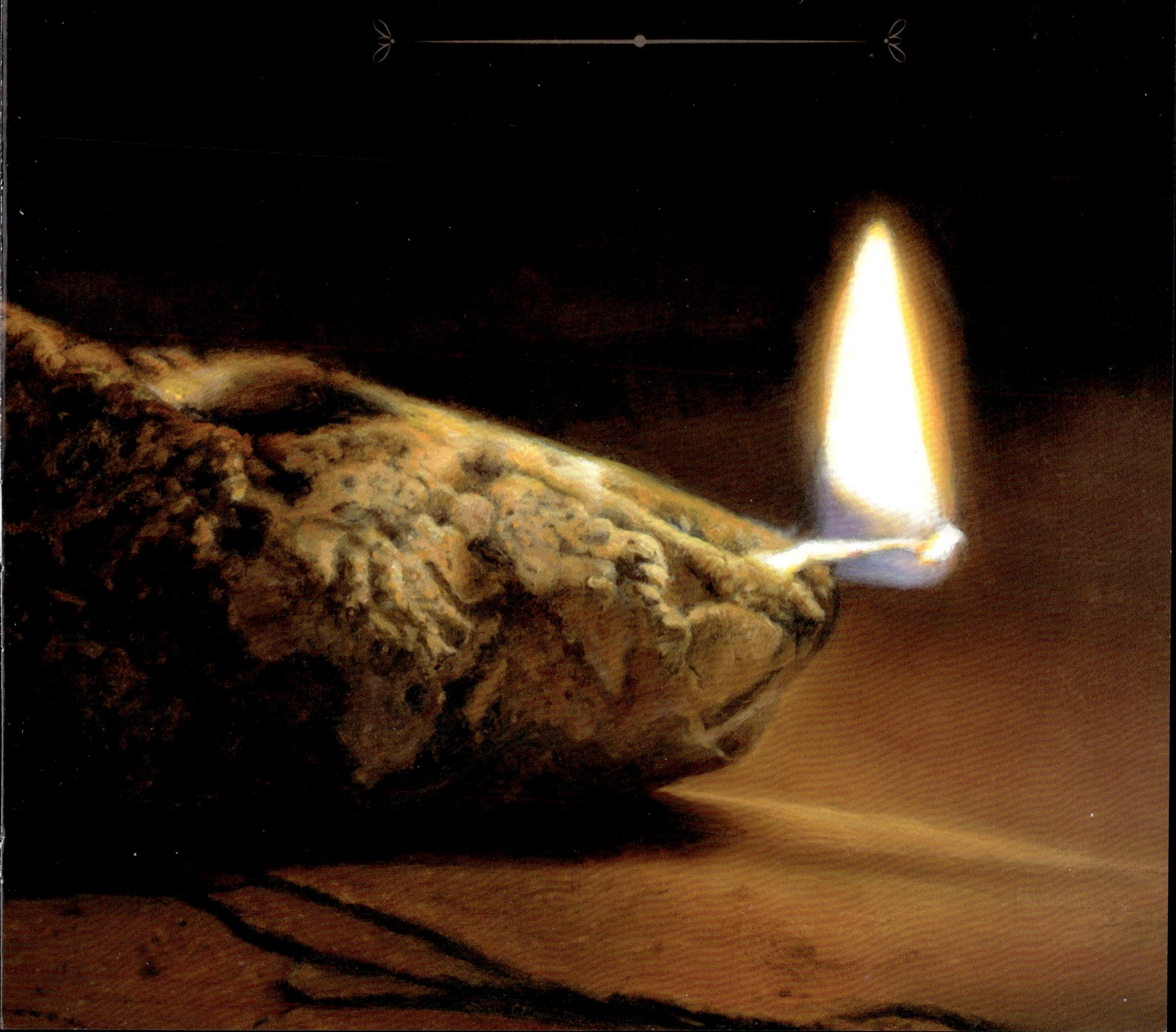

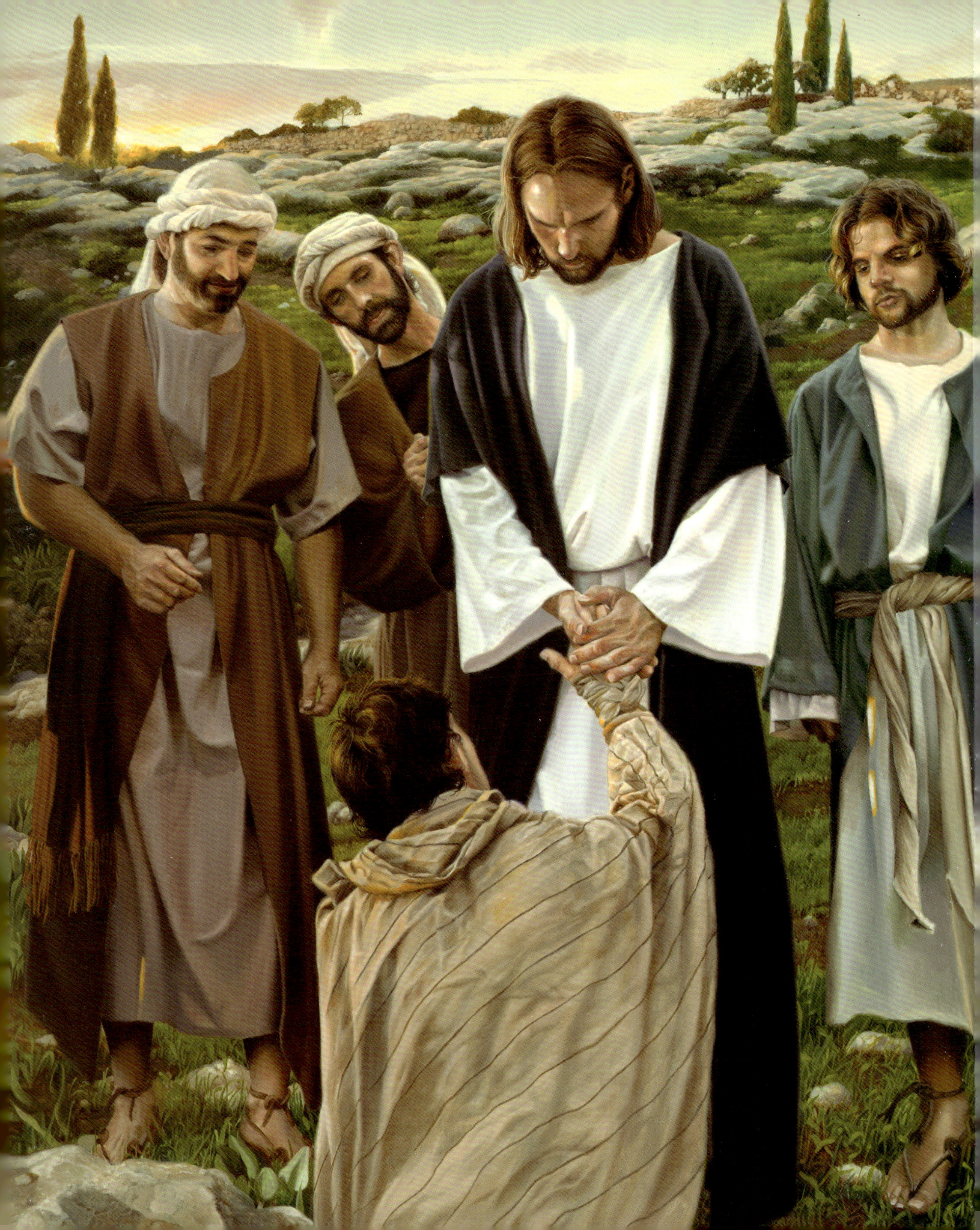

Where Are the Nine?

How often does it seem there is no time for gratitude? The children need to catch the bus, we have to get to the office, we need to run to the store. We have constant daily demands on our time. On the other hand, how time consuming is it to speak the simple words, "Thank You"?

And Jesus answering said, Were there not ten cleansed? But where are the nine? There are not found that returned to give glory to God, save this stranger. And he said unto him, Arise, go thy way: thy faith hath made thee whole.

- Luke 17:17-19

When Christ healed the ten lepers, only one of them came back to give thanks. This one leper reminds us there is *always* time for gratitude.

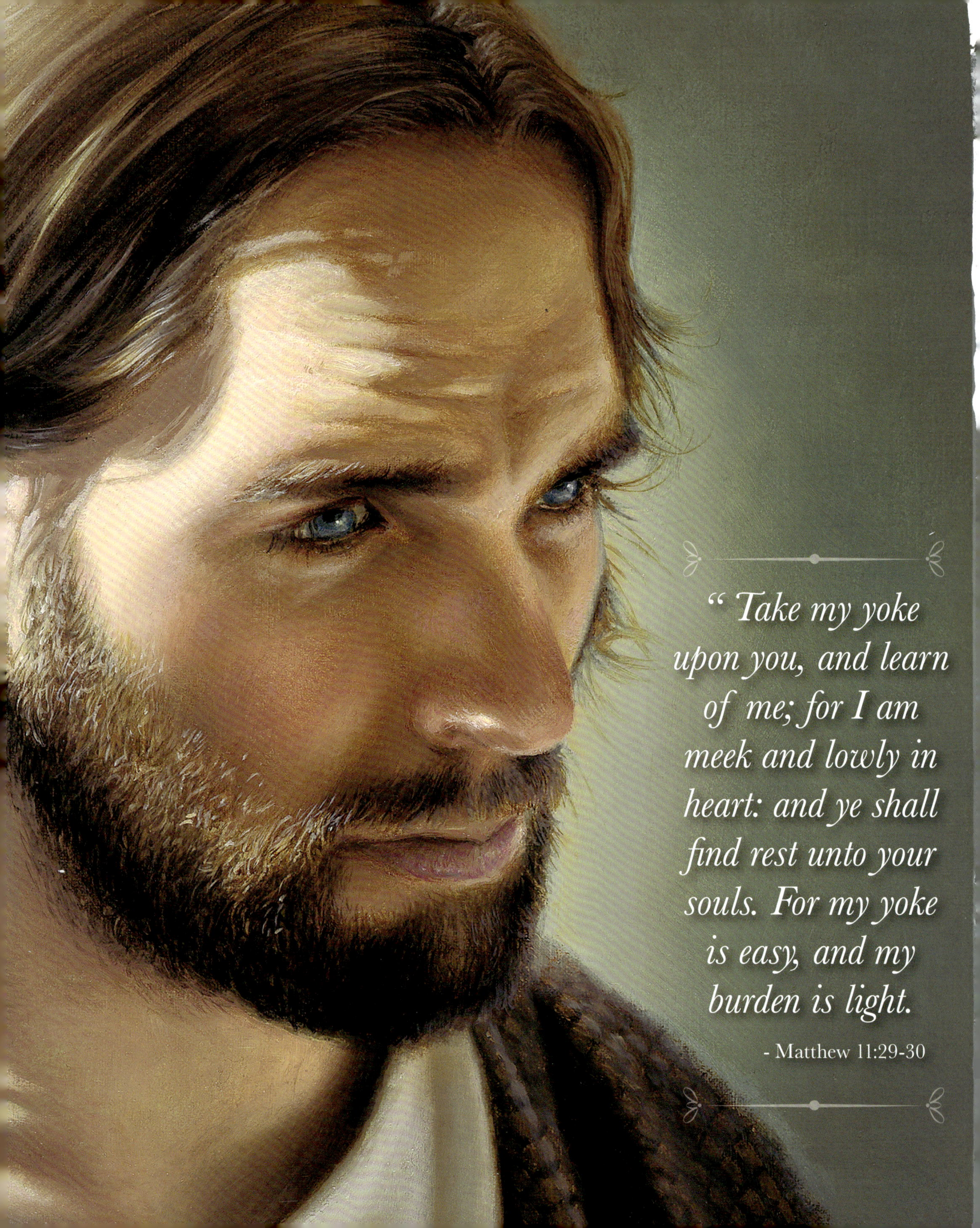
" Take my yoke
upon you, and learn
of me; for I am
meek and lowly in
heart: and ye shall
find rest unto your
souls. For my yoke
is easy, and my
burden is light.
- Matthew 11:29-30